THE BATTLE OF THE BOYNE

by

Enda O Boyle

Duleek Historical Society

Reprinted 1992, 1997, 2000

ISBN No. 0904091 02 3 "The Battle of the Boyne" (pbk)

Cover Design by Una O Boyle

Excel Printing Ltd.
Boyne House, Church Hill, Navan, Co. Meath.

CONTENTS

INTRODUCTION

"July the first, of a morning clear
One Thousand six hundred and ninety
King William did his men prepare –
Of thousands he had thirty –
To fight King James and all his host,
Encamped near the Boyne Water".

THUS BEGAN an old song which describes the events which took place at Oldbridge three hundred years ago. In the pages which follow we shall attempt to reconstruct the details of the battle from contemporary reports, some of which were written within days of the event, and which give detailed accounts of the action as seen from both sides, as well as from books written on the subject.

The most detailed accounts are from Williamite sources, Rev. George Story, who was chaplain to Lord Drogheda's regiment, writes in detail about the whole Williamite campaign in "A True and Impartial History", published in London in 1691. The activities of the Danish force are dealt with in "The Danish Force in Ireland, 1690 – 1691" by Kevin Danaher and J. G. Simms, while the latter describes the happenings in "Eyewitnesses to the Boyne" published in "The Irish Sword" in 1963. On the Jacobite side the principal records come from King James's Memoirs, which are quoted at length in "The Battle of the Boyne" by D. C. Boulger, and from the French accounts of the Irish campaign. These and many other sources have been used in an effort to piece together the events of that fateful day in 1690, and of the period leading up to it.

This account of the battle is aimed at giving the reader a simple straightforward description of the events which took place on July the first, 1690.

BACKGROUND

To understand the background of the Battle of the Boyne it is necessary to delve deeper into the history of Ireland, England and Europe, and particularly that of France in the years preceding 1690.

The very roots of this battle go back to the Reformation, following which Christianity in Europe was divided into those who supported the reformed faith and those who remained loyal to the Papacy. Unfortunately these two elements of the Christian faith were unable to live together and states became Catholic or Protestant, depending on the faith of their rulers - this, in turn was usually followed by non-acceptance, and indeed, persecution of adherents of the opposing form of the faith. In general, the states of southern Europe remained Catholic while the more northern states became Protestant, and in almost every case those who opposed the religion of the state were to find themselves deprived of their rights, and quite frequently having to undergo persecution for the sake of their religion. The one European country which stood out in its tolerance of opinions contrary to that of the state, was France, where in 1598 Henry IV issued the Edict of Nantes whereby Protestants in the Calvanist tradition, called Huguenots, were granted freedom of religious expression. In England and in Ireland it was the complete opposite where supporters of the Papacy became second rate citizens. These two situations were to be influential in later years in the struggle for dominance in Europe by France and in the succession to the English throne. In the case of the latter the Battle of the Boyne was to be the deciding factor, while in France the ever increasing power of Louis XIV was to lead to war which would involve opponents for the English throne on opposite sides.

Louis XIV came to the throne of France in 1643 at the age of 16. Under his reign it became a very powerful country as neighbouring states and provinces were annexed to strengthen the borders of the country which was now threatening to dominate Europe. In 1672 the Spanish Netherlands (Belgium) were captured and Louis turned his attention to Holland, a country which he hated because it was Protestant and he looked down on it because it had no king, being governed by traders. Holland resisted and rallied round the House of Orange for leadership, and elected Prince William as Stadtholder or Governor of the United Provinces. For the next 30 years William was to work and scheme and organise European opposition to Louis as he became leader of the League of Augsburg, a union of most of the other European states which set out to stem the growing threat of the power of the now mighty France.

Louis now turned his attention to matters at home, and wishing to make himself the great Catholic monarch of a great Catholic country, he began to interpret rather strictly the terms of the Edict of Nantes, thus restricting the activities of the French Huguenots, and eventually in 1685 he revoked the edict altogether. The result of this was that to profess Huguenot opinions became a legal crime, and Huguenots were to suffer persecution for their beliefs. Thousands fled the country, going to the German states, Holland, England, Ireland and even further afield to America. The numbers who fled France are variously given as anything from 80,000 to 300,000, and this proved to be a great loss to the country as they took with them their money; and most important of all, these were the skilled artisans in France who were especially noted for their skills in weaving, lace, pottery, silk and glass making - skills which the economy of France could little afford to lose.

Among those who fled was Friedrich Herman, Duke of Schomberg, who was later to oppose James at the Boyne.

Let us now examine the situation in England, which supported the Reformation, and which carried out a policy of persecution against those who were opposed to it. During the period of the Commonwealth, when Oliver Cromwell was Lord Protector, Catholics were bitterly oppressed. In Ireland, in particular, many of the great Catholic estates were confiscated and handed over to Protestant settlers. The death of Cromwell brought great rejoicing in England with the restoration of the monarchy. Charles II became King, but very few of the estates were returned to their original owners - he was obliged to allow the plantations remain as they were, in order to win the support of those who supported Cromwell. In Ireland this was a source of great disappointment where many of the old Catholic families supported the Stuarts in the hope of regaining their lands - unfortunately they were to be disappointed.

Charles died in 1685 and was succeeded by his brother James, who outwardly supported the Catholic faith and did all in his power to restore it. He was anxious to restore the rights of English Catholics and he had a similar policy for Ireland. He was instrumental in having Catholics put into positions of power within the state and within the army, besides this he promised to restore estates to those who had lost them in the past. This outlook won him many supporters in Ireland.

From the records of the Drogheda Corporation the following extract is interesting:

"Att a G. A. etc. 14 April 1685

Coronation day of James II

...... it is ordered by this assembly that there shall be a hogs head of wine bought at ye charge of ye Corporacon and hung up neere the Tholsell doore to be drank on that occasion and that there be a barrell of beere with tobacco and pipes given to every foot company to drink ye King's Health and this to be paid for at ye charge of ye Corporacon and that all aldermen and freemen of ye Corporacon doe attend Mr. Mayor at ye Tholsell to waite on ye King's sword from thence to Church."

James appointed Lord Tyrconnell to be his Lord Viceroy in Ireland in 1687. It is interesting to note that as Richard Talbot, he was a member of Lord Preston's army in 1647 at the age of 16, and that two years later he was a member of the garrison which defended Drogheda against the Cromwellian army. He was severely wounded on that occasion and left for dead, but through the help of one of the Cromwellian soldiers he was looked after, restored to health and later helped to escape.

As Viceroy, Tyrconnell set out to carry out the policy of James by reforming the civic councils and by raising an army which would be representative of the majority of the Irish people, that is, one which would include Catholics as well as Protestants.

The corporations of the towns, due to a law passed in Cromwellian times, which required the taking of an oath repugnant to Catholics, were entirely in the hands of Protestants, but Tryconnell's wish was that both Catholic and Protestant should sit side by side on these councils. However, when he requested this arrangement he was met with the reply "Here are our charters" - the Cromwellian charters which limited membership to Protestants. Acting on behalf of King James, Tyrconnell withdrew these charters, and most councils agreed, but there were protests from Dublin and Derry. Of the latter James had this to say: "There was no trouble except at Londonderry (a stubborn people as they appeared to be afterwards), who stood an obstinate suit, but were forced at last to undergo the same fate as the rest". Having recalled the charters James issued new ones which would allow both Protestant and Catholic members sit together.

Next Tyrconnell turned his attention to the army. At this stage the Irish army was small, consisting solely of two Protestant regiments under Colonel Lundy and Lord Mountjoy. Catholics were not armed, but almost all adult Protestants were members of the militia and had a musket and sword . In order to redress this situation Tyrconnell raised two regiments of Catholics - one of horse and the other of foot - and sent them to England to be trained. Richard Hamilton was put in command of the horse and a Scot, named Cannon, was in command of the foot. Unfortunately their presence in England proved to be another in a series of events which were to bring about the downfall of James. His enemies suggested that he intended to terrorise England with an Irish army, so that these troops became an embarrassment to him. The presence of the Irish troops, his pro-Catholic tendencies, where he continued to appoint Catholics to positions of power, and eventually the birth of a son, which would ensure the continuation a Catholic royal line, brought about his downfall.

Having laid the foundations Tyrconnell now set about raising a national army to support his King. Accordingly he asked the chiefs of the Irish families to prepare lists of officers and men who might form regiments bearing their names. In this way an army of 50,000 men was prepared - it exceeded all expectations, but it was only an army "on paper", and was completely unarmed and untrained.

By the time that these men had been called up and received some initial training news had arrived about the landing of William in England. Tyrconnell now felt that the two Protestant regiments should be moved to a part of Ireland where they would have little influence, and so he ordered Mountjoy and the two regiments to Derry to strengthen the garrison there.

When a son was born to James and Mary of Modena in June of 1688 it brought matters to a head. It had always been assumed that on the death of James he would be succeeded by his daughter, Mary, who was married to William of Orange, but the birth of a son changed all this, as it meant that his son was now first in line to the throne, a fact that would ensure the continuation of the Catholic line and Catholic power on the throne of England.

JAMES II

(Portrait by Sir Godfrey Kneller)

Another important event in the summer of that year finally sealed the fate of James. The country was on the verge of civil war as seven Anglican bishops protested against the powers which James was exercising in order to restore Catholic supremacy. They were tried for treason, but were declared "not guilty". This decision was greeted with demonstrations of celebration at the release of the bishops and shortly after that the first steps were taken to remove James from the throne.

A letter was sent to William

in the names of several English lords and bishops, asking him to come to England to take over the throne from his father-in-law. William gathered an army and landed at Tor Bay on November 5, 1688. The affairs of England and Europe now begin to come closer together. When Louis invaded the German Palatinate in September 1688, the forces of the League of Augsburg united against him. By now they had gained the support of the Pope, Innocent XI, who had his own quarrel with Louis, and who had no desire to see France so mighty that it would dominate all Europe. The arrival of William in England in November deprived Louis of his only ally, James II, and at the same time it meant that he was unable to give James any military help in order to help him to maintain his position. On the positive side for Louis was the fact that William in England was of far less trouble to him than he would have been had he remained in Holland to direct the war against France.

Despite the arrival of William in England, James did not yet feel under any great pressure. He felt that his army of 40,000 was sufficient to enable him to keep the reins of power. However, by early December he found his position untenable and he decided to flee the country. His wife Mary and his son, together with a party of 26 sailed for France on the night of December 10, while James made arrangements to follow later. His departure was fixed for the next night, but his flight was interrupted and he was forced to return to London where much to his surprise and to that of William he was greeted with "bonfires, ringing of bells and all imaginable marks of love and esteem which made it look more like a day of triumph than humiliation". William sent the Dutch Guards under Count Solmes to turn out the King's Guards at Whitehall. James succumbed and arrangements were made afresh for a new departure, which was done with the help of William. Accordingly James left England on December 24 to join his wife Mary at the court of Louis in Paris shortly afterwards.

In Ireland Tyrconnell was in command of the greater part of the country and it was obvious that the only hope that James had of recovering his throne lay there, where 5/6 of the people were still loyal to him, and accepted him as their rightful king.

From James's own point of view Ireland was to be a stepping stone on the way to recovering his lost throne. He had no wish to be an Irish King - England, France and Scotland were all familiar to him, but he was completely unfamiliar with Ireland. In Paris he was the guest of his cousin, Louis, and lived entirely on his good will. He set up court in the palace of St. Germains and from there he maintained his position as legal king of England, although ruling from exile. As regards the court, it was one set up on very frugal lines and offered no encouragement to those who might wish to serve him.

In England William and Mary were pronounced joint monarchs, but not before a prolonged debate in parliament decided so. One of the earliest acts of William was to convene parliament, and the major question before it was to make a decision on the ruler of the country. There were divided opinions, one of which proposed by the Earl of Clarendon, Mary's uncle, was that James should remain king in name only and that William should act as regent: another proposal was that Mary should be Queen, again with William as regent. However, the matter was finally decided with the agreement that William and Mary should rule as joint monarchs. Parliament presented a Declaration of Rights to William and Mary, in which the misrule of James was cited, and listed the controls which the parliament would now exercise over the joint monarchs. The terms were accepted and on February 13, 1689 they were declared King and Queen of England.

In Europe Louis XIV was engaged in war with his opponents of the League of Augsburg, following his invasion of the Palatinate. It suited Louis that the principal leader of the League, William, should be occupied with establishing himself as ruler in England, and it would further assist Louis if James could be persuaded to go to Ireland to seek to regain his throne, and at the same time keep William engaged in a war well away from the European campaign.

In Ireland Tyrconnell was in control of most of the country - with the exception of certain sections of the north. He continued with his efforts to raise an army for James, which would be of assistance to him in his efforts to regain power. Derry and Enniskillen now became rallying points for those who supported

William - among these was Lord Mountjoy, the best general in Ireland, together with his regiment which has already been mentioned. Tyrconnell recognised the danger and had Mountjoy sent to Paris to James, on the pretext that he should advise him to make the best terms he could with William as he had no hope of opposing him successfully. This was Mountjoy's own opinion but the emissary who accompanied him, the Lord Chief Baron, Sir Stephen Rice, told James that Ireland was loyal to him and advised him to prevent Mountjoy from returning. Thus it was that he was sent to the Bastille where he remained for the next three years, unable to take any part in the struggle in Ireland.

JAMES IN IRELAND

Pressure was now being put on James to go to Ireland where Tyrconnell said he had an army to help him, and from which position he might be able to mount a campaign which would restore him to his throne. As for Louis, he saw that it would be greatly to his advantage to extend the war to Ireland and thus weaken his opponents on the continent. Thus it was that on March 12, 1689 James left the port of Brest to arrive at Kinsale two days later. He was met by Tyrconnell who informed him that he had an army of 80,000 ready to fight for him, but that they were badly armed. The poor condition of the troops, arms and money available, were not very encouraging to a king in search of a lost throne, yet James says that he found "a great deal of goodwill in the Kingdom, but little means to execute it". He was pleased with the efforts of the Lord Viceroy, and raised him to the rank of Duke as a reward for his services. It was pointed out to James that he could become King of Ireland, but for his part he made it clear that he had come to regain his English throne, a situation which Tyrconnell sees as a lost cause for many years.

James reached Dublin on Palm Sunday, March 24, and received a tremendous welcome. He was greeted by the Lord Mayor, the Aldermen and the garrison. Bells rang out, and cannons roared in welcome for the King, for this was the first occasion since

1299 when Richard II arrived, that Dublin was to welcome a king.

Meanwhile the Protestants of Derry and Enniskillen had declared for William and Lieutenant Richard Hamilton led an army of 7,000 men against them. Hamilton had been sent over to Ireland in January, as William urged him to discuss terms of settlement with Tyrconnell when rumours spread that the latter would be willing to make some settlement with William. Hamilton accepted the mission, and he gave an undertaking that he would not go over to the Jacobite cause or join their forces. On reaching Ireland he threw in his lot with Tyrconnell and played a major part in the Jacobite campaign.

Derry resisted all efforts in a memorable siege which lasted 105 days and which ended on July 31. Even the arrival of James at the Walls of Derry was not enough to break the spirit of those within the city, who were led by the gallant Rev. George Walker, who was later killed at the Battle of the Boyne.

The Jacobites withdrew leaving Ulster in Williamite hands. The Williamite cause was further strengthened when Marshal Schomberg landed at Bangor. Co. Down on August 13 with an army of 10,000 men. These were joined by the Ulster Corps of Derry and Enniskillen to raise the total strength to 16,000. Having captured Carrickfergus, Schomberg marched south to confront the Jacobite army. At this point there was an opinion expressed in James's camp that many members of Schomberg's army could be induced to desert, and so a proclamation was issued from Drogheda offering every soldier who deserted forty shillings and every officer a commission of equal rank. The proclamation appears to have fallen on deaf ears as there is no record of any great desertions from Schomberg's army at that point.

When James heard of the arrival of Schomberg and of his gathering together a large army in Ulster, he ordered his army to cross the Boyne and march northwards, declaring that he was not going to be walked out of Ireland without striking a blow for it. He assembled all the surrounding garrisons and succeeded in gathering an army of 20,000 men at Ardee by mid-September. By the beginning of October he had come face to face with Schomberg's army on marshy ground just north of Dundalk. But that was the end of it . Neither side felt like engaging in battle and so each returned to their winter quarters. Schomberg had been urged by William to attack the Jacobite forces, but he replied stating that he was faced by an army almost double his, and that it was better equipped, better disciplined and better nourished. Whatever about the opinions he expressed, he felt that his army was not yet ready to face the army of James. Already his men were dying from disease as they lay in camp near Dundalk. On the other hand James, too, did not appear ready for battle, so each side withdrew to their respective winter quarters.

For the Jacobites it was a winter of discontent, as lack of money, bad food, lack of good medical supplies and a general feeling of disappointment with James for not accepting the challenge at Dundalk, led to uneasiness among the troops, which in turn led to quarrelling, and duels became common. The main body of the Jacobite troops was stationed at Ardee, and in spite of the conditions and discontent there was a certain degree of optimism, despite the disappointment of not taking advantage of the situation at Dundalk.

On the other hand Schomberg's army seems to have suffered more as disease and the harsh rigours of an Irish winter played havoc with the men. At Dundalk about 2,000 died from disease, and thousands more died in the winter which followed as they were stricken with dysentery, typhus and influenza. He lost almost half his men during that winter; however, he received reinforcements of about 7,000 Danish troops on March 13. These landed at Belfast and were quartered in Counties Antrim and Derry until the arrival of William later that year. These Danish troops were under the command of Ferdinand Wilhelm, Duke of Wurtemberg, and these too suffered many of the discomforts which afflicted Schomberg's troops.

James, too, received reinforcements, although in his case it was more of an exchange than receiving extra help from France. He had been pressing Louis to sent troops to assist in his Irish campaign, and arrangements were eventually make whereby 7,000 infantry under Count Lazun, were to be sent to Ireland in exchange for the Mountcashell Brigade of 5,387 men. These had earlier been sent to France and were to be the beginning of the famous Irish Brigade within the French army. Lazun and his men landed at Cork on March 12. Lazun himself reached Dublin soon afterwards, while his men followed and pitched camp on the Curragh of Kildare.

WILLIAM III

(Portrait by W. Wissing)

At the end of a long drawn out winter the opposing sides were becoming active again. In February a detachment of Williamite troops under Brigadier William Wolseley captured Cavan. The Williamite cause was heartened by the arrival of the Danish troops in March. Charlemont in Co. Armagh was taken in April and now there was news of the long awaited arrival of William and his army. William was beginning to feel that Schomberg did not display the necessary qualities of leadership to mount a campaign and bring it to a successful conclusion, so he arranged to come over himself and bring with him an army of 20,000 men. These arrived at Carrickfergus on June 14, and with the addition of Schomberg's army and the Danes it brought the Williamite strength up to 36,000.

William's entry to Belfast was no less triumphant than that of James to Dublin over a year previously. He rode into the city in a coach supplied by Schomberg as soldiers, colonists and the general populance came out to greet him. The Mayor and Corporation of Belfast met him, and also there, was Rev. George Walker who had led the defence of Derry, and was now giving support to the great occasion. Bonfires were lit and guns were discharged to signal a royal welcome for King William who was to be their saviour from the unpopular King James.

The stage was set for the confrontation which would decide who should rule as King of Great Britain and Ireland, and whether the line of monarchs should be of the Catholic or Protestant faith.

William now summoned the remaining troops which had been stationed throughout Ulster at Derry, Enniskillen and Newry and elsewhere, to bring his total force up to 54,000. He attended church service in Belfast for the success of the campaign, while at home in the province of Orange he had a Catholic mass celebrated.

As had been mentioned earlier the Jacobites, too, had their spirits lifted with the arrival at Cork of 7,000 troops from France under the command of Count Lazun. It is worth noting that there were very few French represented in this force, it was composed mainly of Swiss, Flemish and Walloons. Shortly after their arrival in Ireland the task of assembling the Jacobite army began. The army which Tyrconnell had drawn up had now received some basic military training from French officers who had come across with James originally, and while they were badly supplied with arms, and horses were scarce, there was a great improvement in their military capabilities. They were mainly stationed between the Boyne and Dundalk and when James rode into camp in Dundalk on June 15, there was an army of over 20,000 assembled there, and with the addition of the French it amounted to over 27,000. They were poorly armed, ammunition was scarce - even the supplies which the French had brought were found to be of poor quality. Thus most of the Irish troops were armed with little more than pikes. For artillery they fared little better, there being only about a dozen cannon, and six more which the French had brought. It took quite a long time to assemble the Irish troops, as can be seen from the fact that Sarsfield did not reach the Boyne until June 25.

William, too, was making ready and assembling his forces. By June 22 he had reached Newry and reviewed the soldiers who were in camp there. When these, and all the other troops at his disposal were assembled he could boast of an army of 36,000 - this was a considerable force and much more than James could muster.

PRELUDE TO THE BATTLE

Just North of Newry there is a pass known as Moyry Pass where the road leading to the Cooley Mountains passes through a marshy region that is capable of being guarded by a relatively small force. In days of old it was known as the Gap of the North which was so ably defended by Cuchulainn against the enemies of Ulster. This marshy area proved just as formidable an obstacle now, and it was here that the first engagement occurred between the Williamite and Jacobite troops. The northern end of this pass had been taken and held by a small force of Williamites, but on the night of June 22, an advance party of Jacobites under Colonel Fitzgerald of Lord Bellew's regiment, and 60 mounted dragoons under Col. Lawrence Dempsey swept down on the 300 English infantry and dragoons who were holding the pass. After a brief little encounter the English were driven back with a loss of 30 men, while the Jacobites lost about 10. Strangely this first victory for the Jacobites proved rather disastrous for them. Among those taken prisoner was a Captain Farlowe who was known to James from his days as king. Farlowe was brought to James and he gave him much misleading information - information which brought dismay to James and caused him to change his plans. Farlowe said that William had an army of 50,000 troops, all highly disciplined and well trained, that these were to flank Dundalk on the West and that a fleet of ships had orders to sail down the coast to Drogheda and so cut off the Jacobites in that direction. James took fright. He felt his army could not stand the double threat of the Williamite army and fleet, and fearing that he might be cut off and surrounded he decided that it would be in his best interests to retreat and make a stand at the Boyne where he would be in a better position to defend Dublin.

It is generally agreed that with the initial success James was in a good position to follow up a successful campaign and there was a feeling of disappointment among his officers when he decided to retreat from what was considered a position of strength. James felt that the Boyne offered a better position on which to make a stand for the defence of Dublin, so orders were given to quit their positions and move southwards. The withdrawal from Dundalk was completed by June 24, and the Jacobite army was on the march towards the Boyne.

Advance parties of Williamites soon brought word to William that the Jacobites were quitting their positions at Dundalk. The pursuit began as the latter retreated towards Ardee. Letters from the Duke of Wurtemberg to King Christian V of Denmark, and to Jens Harboe, his Secretary of War describe the situation.

To the King: "Dundalk 28, 1690. the army had marched in two sections. The King had taken the Nury route. Your Majesty's troops assembled at Armagh........the enemy had encamped with a corps of 10,000 men between Nury and Dundalk with the intention of contesting the defiles; but when he realised we were marching by two routes he retreated as far as Arde. Before that a detachment of foot was detailed to reconnoitre the enemy in the mountains, but as there was a thick mist they were ambushed. 40 or 50 were cut down including two captains......the enemy after fortifying Dundalk against our attack abandoned the town without burning it. Towards evening the entire cavalry and dragoons were ordered to march by night as the King wished to attack the enemy at Arde. But a party which had been sent out and had charged King James's rearguard brought back some prisoners; they said that Arde had been abandoned, and so the order was countermanded and we had a day of rest. Tomorrow we shall march for Drogheda."

To Harboe : "Dundalk, June 28, 1690. The army is now assembled here. The enemy yield everywhere; if they go on like this we shall soon be in Dublin. There was an attempted mutiny in Donlop's regiment because they were not properly paid. I ordered a courtmartial and one man was shot."

The Jacobites reached Ardee by June 28, and scarcely had they left the town than a troop of Williamite horse rode in after them. The withdrawal continued towards the Boyne which they reached the following day. Here James decided he had to make a stand, while he may not have been entirely satisfied with the position he was now in a situation where he had to force the issue at the Boyne or else give up Dublin altogether.

In his Memoirs he says :
"What induced the King to hazard a battle on this inequality was that if it did not there he must lose all without a stroke, and be obliged to quit Dublin and all Munster, and so be reduced to the province of Connaught, where having no magazines he could not subsist very long, it being the worst corn country in Ireland. Besides his men seemed desirous to fight, and being now raised would have been disheartened still to retire before an enemy and see all their country taken from them without one blow for it. and by consequence be apt to disperse and give all for lost."
Despite what James had to say, had he fallen back behind the line of the Shannon it is accepted that he could have held out for years, but he had no wish to spend so much time in such inhospitable country, as he has described.

THE BOYNE

The Jacobite army of about 26,000 crossed the Boyne in two columns on Sunday, June 29 - most of the infantry passed over at Drogheda while the cavalry passed over at Oldbridge. Lazun says: "The infantry marched over the ford at low tide, the drummers beating their drums without having to lift them over their knees". They drew up their troops on the hills overlooking the river. Opinions varied about the prospects for the coming battle. James himself said that the post itself was an indifferently good one, and indeed the country afforded no better - he knew he was in a weak position and had no alternative to risking a battle there. On the other hand Lazun felt that it was not possible to put up a resistance, as the fords were passable everywhere. One of his officers, Lieutenant General Lery asserted that the position was good and the most advantageous for a battle that could have been selected between Dundalk and Dublin. Despite these contrasting opinions this was the site on which James was to risk all in an effort to salvage something from the Irish campaign, and to prevent Dublin falling into Williamite hands.
The Williamites continued their march southwards and reached the northern slopes of the Boyne on June 29. William had about 36,000 men under his command and these troops were

positioned on the high ground overlooking the river while they set up their headquarters at Mellifont Abbey. The march southwards had not been without incident. A Danish diarist describes how two spies were found with two pounds of arsenic for poisoning the water. They were captured and cut to pieces by the English, while Rev. George Story, chaplain to Lord Drogheda's regiment describes how "some of our dragoons went into a house, where they found about 200 scythes stretch'd out on beams, which the Irish either forgot, or had no time to carry over, they brought one of them to the King, who smiled and said it was a desperate weapon".

Story goes on:

"A little way further there was a hill, to the east of the enemie's camp, and North from the town; upon this His Majesty went, from whence he could see the town and all the enemie's camp which lay to the west of the town, all along the river in two lines, here His Majesty had a great deal of discourse with the Prince, Duke Schomberg, Duke of Ormond, Count Solmes, Major General Scravemore, My Lord Sidney and other great officers, who were all curious in making their observations upon the enemy. Major General Scravemore called them 'un petit Armee' (for we could not reckon about five or six and forty regiments that lay encamped). His Majesty answered, that they might have a great many men in town, that there was also a hill to the south west, beyond which they might have men encamped, and that possibly they did not shew all their numbers, however, he said he was resolved to see very soon what they were."

The hill from which William viewed the scene was Tullyesker Hill, just north of Drogheda, and from thence he rode with some of his officers towards the Boyne. By now the Jacobites had mounted three batteries of guns on the hills overlooking the fords and for a time harassed the Willliamites as they were drawing up in positions north of the river. "Here the English stood the shot of the enemy every man on foot by his horse several hours while there passed 200 shots". As they had not been given orders to retire they were forced to hold their positions in the face of this enemy fire. Afterwards William is alleged to have said "Now I see my men will stand".

A Danish view of the situation says:
"As we came near Drogheda, within a mile, we saw the enemy's camp. His troops had marched out properly divided in brigades and were posted very advantageously on the other side of the river. The crossing a little way off was strongly held by the enemy".
According to Story the first of the Williamite guns did not arrive till three o'clock when they were set up " on a furry bank over against the pass". Having mounted them in position they replied to the earlier Jacobite bombardment. He says the first shot killed an officer and a later one destroyed one of the Jacobite guns. After that those troops and horse which were near the river moved uphill towards the summit of the hill, while the bombardment continued from both sides. A shot fell near King James's tent where he had been discussing plans for the battle with some of his officers. This was obviously quite close to the river, and with the danger from the Williamite guns ever growing, it was decided to move away from the river and out of the range of fire. Thus it was that the Jacobite headquarters were set up in the old ruined church near the crest of the hill.
Not long after this William, together with Prince George, Prince of Darmstadt and several other officers went down to the bank of the river to study the tides and to make observations on the army drawn up on the opposite side. He noted the marshy ground on the far side of the river, together with the small houses opposite, which had been fortified and which concealed many gunners there. There were also trenches being dug there, but on account of the earlier bombardment had not been completed. Satisfied with the situation, William made up his mind that it was here he was determined to force his way across, and then he rode upstream for about 200 yards and there he got off his horse and sat down on the grass for some time to refresh himself. About this time Story says that five gentlemen of the Irish army rode along the opposite bank, so close were they that it was possible to hear their comments on the Williamites as they marched into positions. Those officers were named as the Duke of Berwick (James Fitzjames, illegitimate son of James), Lord Tyrconnell, Sarsfield, Parker and Lazun.

Story describes what follows thus:
"Whilst His Majesty sat there we observed five gentlemen of the Irish army, ride softly along the other side, and make their remarks about our men as they marched in. Those I heard afterwards were the Duke of Berwick, my Lord Tyrconnell, Sercefield, Parker, and some say Lazun..... and whilst His Majesty sate upon the grass, being about an hour, there came some of the Irish with long guns, and shot at our dragoons who went down to the river to drink, and some of ours went down to return the favour; then a party of about forty horse, advanced very slowly, and stood upon a ploughed field over against us, for near half an hour, and so retired to their camp; this small party, as I have heard from their own officers since, brought two field pieces among them, dropping them by a hedg on the plow'd land, undiscover'd; they did not offer to fire them, till His Majesty was mounted, and then he and the rest riding softly the same way back, their gunner fires a piece, which killed us two horses and a man about a hundred yards above where the King was, but immediately comes a second, which had almost been a fatal one, for it grazed upon the bank of the river, and in the rising slanted

William was wounded near this point

upon the King's right shoulder, tore out a piece of his coat, and tore the skin and flesh, and afterwards broke the head of a gentleman's pistol."

A Danish account says: "The enemey's cannon then began to make themselves heard. The Prince of Darmstadt's horse was killed, shot through the neck by a cannon ball. Soon afterwards the King was grazed on the right shoulder by a similar ball, so that he received a fairly wide, but not a deep or dangerous wound."

William seemed to dismiss the event by remarking "It could have come nearer". He had the wound dressed and afterwards spent the rest of the evening riding through the camp meeting and encouraging his men. It also served the purpose of assuring them that whatever accident had befallen him, he was none the worst for it and was perfectly fit to lead them into battle on the following day.

The wounding of King William was seen from the south bank and soon the word went round the Jacobite camp that he had been killed. This was followed by great cheering and shouting - the rumour spread to Dublin, and eventually reached Paris before the result of the battle was received. It is said that bonfires were lit there to celebrate the event.

The cannon fire continued through the rest of the day, but it appears that very little damage was done on either side.

The soldiers did not all seem to be committed to the cause for which they were fighting, for we read about desertions from one side to the other. Story says "some deserters came from them to us", and that a Frenchman ran down to the river to go over to the Jacobites. It appears that a crowd ran down to greet him, but a Williamite cannon fired on them "which killed several, and 'twas said the fellow himself". These deserters often brought valuable information with them to the enemy, one of them according to a Danish account, coming across about midnight said that the Jacobites had packed all their baggage and seemed about to withdraw.

Councils of war were held on each side. On the Williamite side Schomberg urged that a false attack should be made at Oldbridge to focus the enemy's attentions on that point, while the main part of the army should be sent four or five miles upstream during the night to cross the river at some fords there, and thus attack from the right. This plan also had the advantage of getting behind the enemy and reaching Duleek before them in order to control the bridge over the River Nanny there. At this point the Nanny was very marshy and could be crossed only by a narrow bridge, which had been built by William Bath and Janet Dowdall of Athcarne Castle in 1587, and which could be crossed by only one carriage at a time, while Story says : "there is only one place to get across and there not above six can go abreast". This became the focal point of the battle - if the Williamites could hold the Pass of Duleek, then the Jacobites would find themselves caught between the Boyne and Duleek and would be forced to fall back on Drogheda, and in so doing would have to give up Dublin. This was a bold plan of Schomberg's, but the Dutch general, Count Solmes, opposed it and urged that a crossing should be attempted at Oldbridge in the teeth of the enemy. This appealed to William as the more daring plan, but yet he considered it risky and decided to compromise between the two. So it was decided to make use of both sets of proposals. Schomberg's son, Count Meinhard Schomberg, with a force of cavalry and dragoons amounting to about 10,000 was to move to the right to attempt a crossing at the fords at Rosnaree while the main thrust of the army would force the river crossing at Oldbridge. Having got his point accepted Schomberg now urged that the movement to the right should be made that evening in order that they might take the Jacobites by surprise and effect a crossing either before midnight or in the early hours of the morning. Whether this appealed to William or not, it made no difference. He refused to agree to this early movement of troops to the right before midnight as, on account of a long held superstition, he would never undertake anything of importance on a Monday. As a result this flanking movement did not take place until next morning. In the meantime preparations were being made for the attack on the fords at Oldbridge which was to take place at about ten o'clock next morning when the waters would be at their lowest, at low tide. William rode through he camp that night urging his men to the great events that lay before them in the morning. Each man was told to put a sprig of leaves in his hat in order to distinguish him from the enemy who would be wearing pieces of paper to resemble the white cockade of France. This arrangement was necessary as there was no standard uniform and in the thick of the fighting it would be difficult to distinguish friend from foe. To add to this difficulty of distinguishing the opposing sides in the course of the fighting, many of the opposing regiments wore uniforms that were hard to distinguish from one another.

Meanwhile on the Jacobite side a council of war was also held. As has been mentioned earlier, opinions were divided on the possibility of defending the position. James was determined to make a stand, but in this he was opposed by Lazun and Tyrconnell. As for Lazun it appears that, acting under the orders of Louis XIV, he was more concerned with prolonging the war in Ireland and thus keeping William out of affairs on the continent, so he was more inclined to act defensively than to risk a battle which might prove decisive one way or the other and thus bring about an end to the campaign in Ireland. From a military point of view Tyrconnell was opposed to a confrontation, he felt that the river was too easily fordable and that the Jacobites would soon find themselves in a weaker position. Lery who commanded the French cavalry considered the position extremely favourable to the Jacobites and sided with James, urging that a stand should be made. For James's part he may not have been too enthusiastic, but he felt that having retreated from Dundalk when his men were anxious to press ahead, he now felt obliged to make a stand at the Boyne rather than face the ignomy of losing it all without a stroke, as he mentioned earlier. This was not the frame of mind in which one should face up to a battle which he realised would be decisive in his efforts to regain his throne.

It is difficult to determine what decisions were made at the Jacobite council of war. There are indications that preparations were made to defend Oldbridge, while on the other hand there are indications that the Jacobites were about to withdraw from the site.

A Danish diary, mentioned before, says: "About midnight a

deserter came in, who reported that the enemy had struck all his tents and sent off his baggage, so that there was every sign that he was about to withdraw". This may indeed have been so, it also might have been that preparations were being made to clear the site for the battle which was to take place.

There seems to be confirmation of this decision to retreat in a report from Nicholas Plunkett (a Jacobite) who had this to say: "The King resolved in the evening on Monday to decamp that night, but unhappily again that resolution was not executed till Tuesday morning, July 1, at eight o'clock, at which time the army was commanded to March upwards by the river, giving their right flank to the enemy in order, as ' twas believed to go to Dublin to get a better opportunity of defence or of giving battle".

While according to Boulger, writing in 1911 "James held a council of war and it was decided after the army had been assured that a stand would be made, not to fight but to retreat. Unfortunately this intention was not put into immediate practice. It was assumed with that habitual procrastination which had so often proved so fatal to the cause of the Stuarts that there would be time enough in the morning. When morning arrived the baggage was packed up and sent off to Dublin, and with it were sent twelve of James's total of eighteen pieces of artillery".

To add to our speculations that James may have had his mind more on retreating than on making a stand, there is an account which says that on Monday, James in a not very optimistic frame of mind, sent Sir Patrick Trant, First Commissioner of the Revenue, and another Gentleman to Waterford to prepare ships. Thus it appears that even at this stage James may have had his mind set more on leaving the country than on making a stand.

In spite of all this speculation we know that the Jacobites, too, were aware of the dangers of losing control of the Pass of Duleek, and that a flanking movement by the Williamite right could easily cut off that narrow pass, and thus hinder their chances of retreat should such be necessary. Lieut. Gen. Hamilton insisted that efforts should be made to prevent a crossing at this point, and so, Sir Neale O'Neill was sent to the left with a small force of 800 dragoons to guard the fords at

Rosnaree. (Dragoons were foot soldiers who moved from place to place on horseback). Lazun says that this was done on Sunday, But James in his Memoirs says that it was done on June 29 (Monday). The regiments of Lords Antrim and Clanrickard were posted to defend the fords at Oldbridge, while Drogheda was held by Lord Iveagh with 1,300 men.

It is difficult to understand what James had in mind at Donore on the eve of the battle. What is certain is that he withdrew 12 of the 18 cannon (the other six belonged to the French), and sent them on to Dublin. These were the cannon which carried out a constant bombardment of the Williamites on the previous day, yet now James saw fit to remove them from the field of battle altogether, so that on the day of the battle there was not a single piece of artillery on the Jacobite side at Oldbridge. When James is describing the events at Rosnaree he implies that he would have withdrawn more forces from Oldbridge but for the fact that "the cannon and baggage not being far enugh advanced on their way to Dublin."

JULY 1, 1690

"The day was very clear as if the sun itself had a mind to see what would happen" (Story)

ROSNAREE

The first action of the day was at Rosnaree where Count Schomberg in command of the horse and Lieutenant General Douglas in command of the infantry moved out between five and six o'clock in the morning. Some time between eight and nine Sir Neale O'Neill saw the enemy approach the river across the open spaces between the ancient mound of Newgrange and the Boyne. Realising the fact that his men were so totally outnumbered he immediately sent word to James requesting all the help possible. His small force did what they could but they were unable to prevent the superior forces of Schomberg from crossing the river. Schomberg's adjutant, writing to his wife from Duleek the next day describes what happened there; "He brought his force of cavalry, dragoons, infantry and five small

THE BATTLE OF THE BOYNE *(A contemporary view by Theodor Maas)*

cannon and found the ford guarded by 1200 horse (actual figure about 800). Schomberg sent his 100 mounted grenadiers to the ford to draw the enemie's fire, these were followed by Dutch dragoons. When they reached the ford the enemy began to fire but the dragoons plunged into the river. The enemy charged but the Count observed that the charge had thrown his men into disorder, so sword in hand he led the dragoons across the river so effectively that the enemy was driven back two miles towards the main force at Oldbridge."

Although James was not yet there, he too describes the event from an account given to him later by one of O'Neill's men.

"Sir Neale O'Neil's men did their part very well and disputed the passage with the enemie almost an hour till their cannon came up and then retired in good order with the loss of only five or six common men, but their Colonel was shot through the thigh and an officer or two wounded."

O'Neill was the "Colonel who was shot through the thigh" in that encounter. His loss of blood was great and he died about a week later in Waterford.

When news of this event was brought to James he took fright and, thinking that the main thrust of the Williamite attack was to come from his left, he ordered the French under Lazun and the dragoons of Sarsfield and Major General Thomas Maxwell to go to the assistance of O'Neill to try to stem this movement which threatened his left and also, now that the river had been crossed, the Williamites were nearer to Duleek than the main army at Oldbridge, so that the losing of the Pass of Duleek, which James feared, was now a possibility. James goes on with his account of what happened there:

"No sooner had the enemie passed there but they stretched out their line to the right as if they designed to take us in the flank or get between us and Dublin which Mons De Lausune seeing marched with the left to keep up with them and observe their motion; while this was a-doing the King went to the right to hasten up the troops to follow Lausune believing the main body of the enemie's army was following their right which had passed at Slane, but when the King came up he found the Duke of Tyrconnell with the right wing of the horse and dragoons and the two first brigades of the first line drawn up before old brig, from which post he did not think fit to draw them, the cannon and baggage not being far enugh advanced on their way to Dublin."

It can be seen from this that James seemed to be more concerned with withdrawing the troops from Oldbridge than he was about making a stand there, and but for the fact that the cannon and baggage were not far enough advanced on the way to Dublin, he would have withdrawn all the troops from Oldbridge.

Lieut. General Douglas had been sent with his infantry to augment the Williamite force on the right. He had been ordered to cross at the bridge of Slane; but as this bridge had been broken down earlier by the Jacobites, he crossed at some fords between Slane and Rosnaree to join Schomberg's men who were now well established on the south bank of the river.

The Jacobites had been forced back about two miles towards the main force at Oldbridge, this would place them in the townland of Roughgrange, and near the hill known as the Black Hill which leads up over Corballis and towards Duleek. To the south of the river a long steep bank runs along at this point and beyond it there is a narrow valley through which a small stream runs to enter the Boyne further down. The terrain here seems to have given the opposing sides many problems as each sought to outwit the other in their efforts to gain the pass of Duleek.

Again James describes the situation:

"Then the King rid along the line where he found Lausune and the enemie's right drawn up in battle within half a cannon shot of each other. The King did not think fit to charge just then being in expectation of the troops he had left at old bridg, but while he was discussing this matter with Lausune an aide de Camp came to give the King an account that the enemie had forced the pass at old bridg, and that the right wing was beaten." At this stage James became alarmed lest his opponents should hear the news from Oldbridge, which would urge them on to better things, so he whispered to Lazun that he should now charge the enemy before they should hear what had happened in the centre.

Accordingly the French were drawn up in formation and orders were given to move against the enemy when Sarsfield and

Maxwell who had been examining the ground between the two opposing sides had this to say:
"It was impossible for the hors to charge the enemie by reason of two dubble ditches with high banks on either side and a little brook betwixt them that run along the small valley that divided the two armys and at the same time the enemie's dragoons got on horseback, and their whole line began to march to their right, and we soon lost sight of their van by a village that interposed: only by the dust that ris behind it they seemed to endeavour to gaine Dublin Road. Upon which the King (sins he could not attack them) thought fit to march also by his left towards Dublin road too to pass a small brook at Dulick which was impracticable high up by reason of a bog. The King was no sooner on his march but the right wing's being beat was no longer a mistery for several of the scatter'd and wounded horsemen got among them before they rought Dulick; whereupon Mons de Lausune advised the King to take his own regiment of horse which had the van of that wing, and some dragoons and make the best of his way to Dublin."
Thus it was that the rival forces of the Williamite right and the Jacobite left tried to outwit each other, as each sought to gain control of the vitally important Pass of Duleek. Yet for all the importance of the pass it appears that there was little real military engagement between the sides, and there are no records of any confrontation apart from that one reported by Sarsfield, and although they were prepared to attack, the very nature of the ground prevented it, and afterwards the Jacobites managed to prevent the Williamites by-passing them to gain their objective.

OLDBRIDGE

Meanwhile at Oldbridge the action had already begun. Shortly before ten o'clock the Dutch Blue Guards under their commander Count Solmes began their march down towards the water's edge, with drums beating and fifes playing "Lillebulero". At the water's edge the drums stopped and they marched straight into the river, eight or ten abreast. Either the level of the tides had been misjudged or the very mass of their bodies

formed such a barrier that the water rose above their waists, in contrast to the crossing of the French on Sunday, when according to Lazun: "the drummers beating their drums without having to lift them over their knees".
They marched straight ahead through the water. Across the river in the small village of Oldbridge the houses and gardens were occupied by Jacobite troops who had strengthened these positions by building embankments in front of them. The regiments of Lords Antrim and Clanrickard had been sent to defend the ford, and as the Dutch were about half way across the river a peal of shot rained down upon them from the Jacobite positions. This does not appear to have been very effectual, as Story relates : "The enemy did not fire until our men were towards the middle of the river, and then a whole peal of shot came from the hedges, breastworks, houses, and all about, yet we could not perceive any fall except one, and another stagger'd".
The Dutch pressed on and drew up in two lines on the south bank. These two lines of men fired in turn at their enemies, who were behind the hedges and barricades. The fire proved too much for the Irish and very shortly they quit their positions to move up the hill away from the river bank and to take up new

The Boyne at Oldbridge

positions. In doing so they gave the Dutch the opportunity of getting the rest of their men across the river to form a vital foothold on the south bank, which would be so important in making it easier for the other Williamite forces to make their respective crossings downstream. When Tyrconnell saw what was happening he ordered five infantry regiments under Richard Hamilton to support those already at Oldbridge.

According to the Danish Envoy : "The regiment of the Dutch Guards was the first to cross, the men being above their waists in the water. The enemy occupied a village on the bank about which there are small gardens enclosed by hedges, the Dutch rushed to attack with such impetus that their opponents immediately abandoned their position and our men having pursued them for some time drew themselves up in battle formation to maintain the ground they had gained."

Following this initial success William now directed the French Huguenots under Colonel Caillimote and the Enniskillens and other northern regiments to cross the Boyne about 100 yards downstream from the Dutch, who had now managed to establish themselves over the river. The English under Sir John Hanmer and the Danes were to cross shortly afterwards a little bit further down.

Tyrconnell now committed the main troops of cavalry under the Duke of Berwick and Colonel Hugh Sutherland and Captain Robert Parker in support to try to stem the ever advancing enemy. The cavalry together with the five infantry regiments, together with those of Antrim and Clanrickard now became engaged in a fierce struggle as they tried to prevent a bad situation getting even worse. Story says: "This action began at a quarter past ten, and was so hot till past eleven that a great many old soldiers said they never saw brisker work".

Major Arthur of the Royal Guard led a particularly daring charge against the Dutch, he grabbed a pike from one of his men and drove it through one of their officers. Arthur was wounded in the struggle and he died later from his wounds.

Story again describes the situation thus: "One would have thought that man and horse had risen out of the earth for now there appeared a great many battalions and squadrons of the enemy all of a sudden, who had stood behind the little hills".

Although James was not present at Oldbridge he gives an account of what happened there in his 'Memoirs'. This account was probably supplied to him by Colonel (afterwards General) Dorrington who commanded the Royal Guards. He says: "as for what pass'd at Old Brig, it seems the enemie perceiving the left wing and most of the foot had march'd after Lausun attacked the regiment which was at the village of Old Brig with a great body of foot, all strangers, and soon possessed themselves of it: upon which the seaven battalions of the first line, which were left there and drawn up a little behind the rising ground which shelter'd them from the enemies cannon, marched up to charge them, and went on bouldly until they came within a pike's length of the enemie notwithstanding their perpetual fire, so that Major Arthur who was at the head of the first battalion of the guards run the officer through the body that commanded the battalion he march'd up too. But at the same time the enemies horse began to cross the river which the King's foot perceiving immediately gave way notwithstanding all that Dorington and the other officers could do to stop them which cost several of the Captains their lives as Arundel, Ashton, Dungen, Fitzgerald and two or three more."

With the Williamites now pouring across the river downstream the Jacobites were under severe pressure, and while they were unable to stem this new onrush, they made things very difficult for them. Caillimote, urging his men on, received a fatal blow, and as he was being carried back across the river he continued urging his French Huguenots who had suffered so much under Louis XIV, and who considered his ally, James, and his forces in an equal light. At this stage it appears that Schomberg became concerned about the Dutch, and seeing that they were under great pressure and in danger of failing to maintain the ground they had gained, he crossed the river to help, lead and encourage them. He was 75 years of age and he truly displayed great valour when one of his age was so actively engaged in the thick of the battle. It was an unfortunate venture, for while urging his men on at this point he was killed in one of the military engagements. A lieutenant of Dorington's regiment, named Sir Charles OToole is alleged to have made the fatal blow by striking him with his sword across the neck. No sooner had he fallen than Rev. George Walker rushed to his assistance; he too was killed; he was shot a little way beyond the river. No sooner had he fallen than "he was stripped immediately; For the Scots-Irish who followed our camp were got through already; and took off most of the plunder".

The Danes had most difficulty in crossing. About half a mile down from the position of the initial attack the water was much deeper and they had "to go into the water up their armpits - and some up to their necks - and thereafter climb a high hill". But cross they did. However, no sooner were they across than they were driven back again by a very determined charge of the Jacobite cavalry. The Danish diarist: "The enemy cavalry turned against the regiment of Mellioniere and Hamore (Hanmer) and our cavalry with difficulty got breathing space by the efforts of our right wing. The dragoon regiment was at once driven back, and thus the other enemy brigades were also thrown into confusion and fell back to a high hill. Although the enemy rallied several times and defended himself against our men, he was driven back each time."

While the infantry regiments now made vain attempts to hold back the Williamites, the cavalry charged recklessly in all directions. Tyrconnell's, Parker's, Sutherland's and Berwick's troops of horse made charge after charge against far superior odds, and for a time had the enemy under such pressure that they were unable to extend very much the foothold they had established on the south bank of the Boyne. The Duke of Berwick had a horse shot from under him and "was some time amongst the enemie, he was rid over and ill bruised; however, with the help of a trooper he got off again. Sheldon who had command of the horse, had two killed under him." While Berwick's own account of the Battle of the Boyne states that he and his cavalry "charged and charged again ten times, until the enemy amazed at our boldness halted".

William now decided that the time was right for him to enter the fray. It was about midday and he had just heard of the death of Schomberg, so he felt that he should become actively engaged and give the leadership that had been lost by the death of his general, and to urge his men forward, for despite their superior numbers they were finding it difficult to dislodge the Jacobite force from their positions at Oldbridge. He therefore ordered General Ginkel to lead the Dutch cavalry, together with two regiments of dragoons to cross the river about a mile down from the point where the original attack was made. Again, this was a difficult crossing. Seeing this new onset from Donore Hill, Tyrconnell ordered Lord Dungan and his troop of dragoons against them to try to prevent a further crossing which would leave the Jacobites open from their right. On the north bank William now ordered two cannons to be brought up while the Danish infantry shot volley after volley against the Irish to give cover to the Dutch cavalry as they were crossing. Lord Dungan was killed by one of the first shots and several of his officers were also killed, and many more were wounded in this hail of gunfire. Disheartened at the loss of their commander and some of their officers the rest of the regiment galloped off over the heights of Rathmullen, towards Duleek, and they took no further part in the battle.

William crossed shortly after this. His horse became bogged down in the marshy ground and he was forced to alight. He found himself in some difficulties until, as tradition says, he was helped out of the mud by an Enniskilliner named McKinlay. Having got on to more solid ground he mounted his horse again and drawing his sword helped his men against the enemy.

The wound which William suffered the day before still troubled him - there are conflicting reports about its effects. Story says: "His Majesty drew his sword (which was yet troublesome to him) and marched at the head of them towards the enemy". Lt. Gen. Portland: "William was so crippled that he could hardly hold his sword".

The Earl of Portland says he carried his sword in his left hand, while the Danish Envoy says he carried a walking stick.

In spite of his wound William displayed some fine leadership. His crossing at Drybridge now extended the Williamite front for about a mile and a half along the river, a factor which forced the over extended Jacobites to be further extended. Yet the Jacobite horse charged recklessly on, and Ginkel's regiment was forced to withdraw in a lane to the left. "Ginkel stay'd in the rear of his men (being much vex'd at their retreating) and was in some

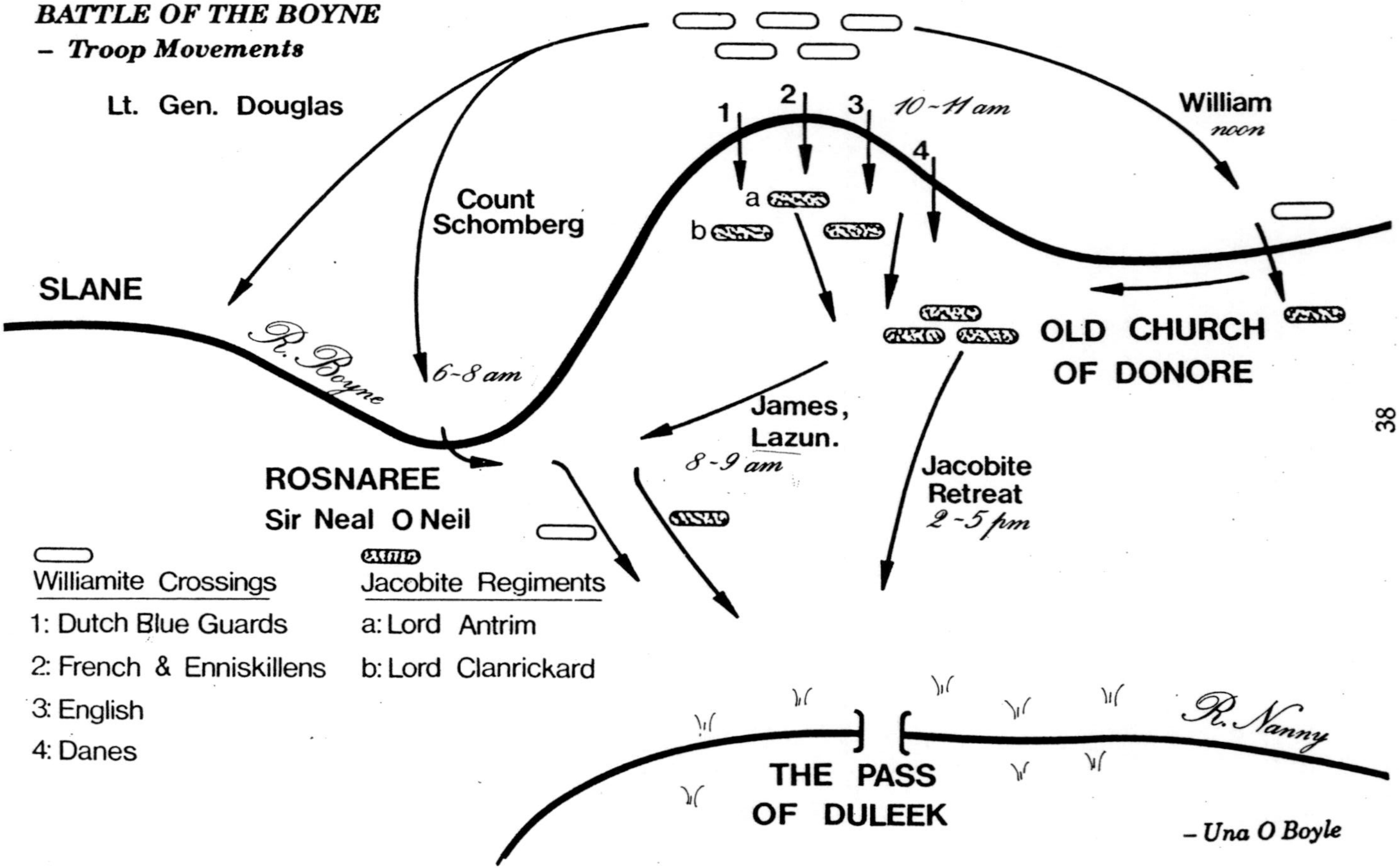
BATTLE OF THE BOYNE
– Troop Movements
Lt. Gen. Douglas
Count Schomberg
6-8 am
SLANE
R. Boyne
ROSNAREE
Sir Neal O Neil
1
2
3
4
10-11 am
a
b
William
noon
OLD CHURCH OF DONORE
James, Lazun.
8-9 am
Jacobite Retreat
2-5 pm
THE PASS OF DULEEK
R. Nanny
Williamite Crossings
1: Dutch Blue Guards
2: French & Enniskillens
3: English
4: Danes
Jacobite Regiments
a: Lord Antrim
b: Lord Clanrickard
– Una O Boyle

danger from our own dragoons, for the enemy being close to him, they could not well distinguish; the dragoons here did a piece of good service in stopping the enemy, (who came up boldly) and our horse rallying both here and to the right, after near half an hour's dispute the enemy were again beat from this place, and a great many of them killed". (Story).

The Jacobites were now overstretched and were unable to contain the assaults against them all along the Boyne. They were forced to give ground, and fell back on the high ground around the old church of Donore where the old walls and the surrounding hedges were lined with men as they made ready to make a final stand. There were wild skirmishes at various points in the fields around. By now most of the distinguishing marks of white paper and green sprigs had been lost and it was difficult to tell friend from foe. A troop of Dutch horse was thrown into confusion as they were unable to distinguish their allies from their attackers. "The place was unfortunately full of holes and dung pits and the passages narrow: but above all the dust and smoak quite blinded them" wrote Sir Robert Southwell. He goes on : "His Majesty was there in the crowd of all, and animating them that fled to follow him. His danger was great among the enemy's guns which killed thirty of the Inniskilliners on the spot. One of the Inniskilliners came with a pistol cocked at his Majesty till he called out 'What, are you angry with your friends?'" Upon recognising him, there was a great cheer from the northern regiment, and William then took over and led them in a charge against the Jacobite positions at Donore. A counter charge by Richard Hamilton and his troop of horse drove the Enniskilliners and the Dutch back for a time: but it was to no avail. It was now mid-afternoon and Tyrconnell saw that further resistance was impossible. He gave orders that a retreat should be made towards Duleek, with the cavalry doing their best to cover the retreating foot soldiers until they got to further safety beyond the River Nanny, where it might be possible to hold up the Williamite pursuit for a while.

In one of the last cavalry charges of the day Richard Hamilton was wounded and taken prisoner. He was brought before William who questioned him about the performance of the Irish, and whether they would fight any more. "Upon my honour, I believe they will" he replied. But William remembered that this was the man whom he had sent to Ireland to make terms with Tyrconnell, on the understanding that he would not go over to the Jacobite cause. That he broke his word to William was a source of annoyance to him, and at the sound of the word 'honour' he looked at him, and repeating the word once or twice, he remarked "Your honour", the accent on the first word implying that Hamilton was not a man of honour.

DULEEK

The pursuit now began, as the Jacobite cavalry fought bravely to cover the retreating foot soldiers as they made their way towards Duleek.

On the left wing of the Jacobites there was also a general movement towards Duleek. Here the French, together with Sarsfield's and Maxwell's dragoons succeeded in keeping the Williamite right from gaining control of the vital pass over the Nanny. However, the action on this wing was in contrast to that which took place at Oldbridge. This appears to have been a battle of wits as each sought to outwit the other, without becoming involved in an actual engagement - a cat and mouse game which continued all afternoon.

In describing events on this sector Story says that they met with great difficulty in the nature of the ground, for there were corn fields, with great ditches, and beyond these there was a great bog. The horsemen went to the right of it, but the infantry were commanded to march through it, and they found this as great a hardship as fighting itself. He felt that the Jacobites lost a great chance there, as he says: "Yet when the enemy saw our men take the bog, instead of charging them in it, they retreated in haste towards Duleek, which Count Schomberg seeing, fell in among their foot and kill'd a great many". Whether Story in mentioning the 'bog' is referring the the "dubble ditches" before mentioned, and the little stream in the valley behind the hills overlooking the Boyne, or to the Commons of Duleek, which would have been more extensive then than it is today, and certainly much wetter, it is hard to say, but I am inclined to the view that this engagement took place on the latter site just before the Jacobites reached Duleek.

It was now about five o'clock and the left wing and the centre of the retreating Jacobites were approaching Duleek at about the same time. There was great confusion as the retreating Irish infantry got among the highly disciplined French who were arriving from Rosnaree. For a time there was complete disorder, and the Jacobites were threatened more from their own confusion, than they were from their enemies. We are told that this took place "between high banks in Duleek lane", Colonel Zurlauben had to fire on the Irish to keep them off and to restore order to a very confused situation. Whether this took place at the crossing over the Nanny or at some other place we do not know, but the French managed to restore order, the cavalry gained control of the pass, and the rest of the army got across the bridge safely.

Shortly before this Lazun advised King James to take his own regiment of horse and make his way as best he could, to Dublin. Thus it was that James together with the dragoons of Sarsfield and Maxwell departed the scene and headed for Dublin. Of the event James says how Lazun "advised the King not to remain at Dublin neither, but to go with all expedition for France to prevent his falling into his enemie's hands ..... that as long as there was life there was hope and that if once he was in France again, his cause was not so desperate".

At Duleek the French placed their remaining five cannon (one had been destroyed, either the previous day at Oldbridge or in the encounter at Rosnaree) on the high ground (The Barr Hill) overlooking the Nanny. The six French infantry regiments, together with the cavalry and dragoons were drawn up to face the Williamites as they arrived, and thus give the Irish infantry the opportunity of getting away from their pursuers. The narrow bridge over the Nanny, together with the boggy nature of the ground made this situation as difficult as crossing the Boyne. The Williamites were brought to a temporary halt.

When the infantry had advanced a safe distance the French and the cavalry continued their retreat towards Dublin. They were followed and there were some minor engagements along the way. "Few or none of the men escaped ... for they shot them like hares amongst the corn, and in the hedges as they found them in their march". When the Williamites got as far as the Naul they were satisfied that there would be no further resistance from the Jacobites, so they returned to Duleek where they spent the night. Of the total casualties that day the Jacobites lost about 1,000 while the Williamites lost about 500.

It was one of those summer nights with clear skies, following a very hot day and it was difficult to keep warm, especially for those who had been fighting all day in wet dirty clothes. They managed to keep the cold at bay and to ease their plight somewhat by making bonfires in Duleek of the guns, pikes and gunpowder which the retreating Irish had thrown away.

But guns and pikes were not the only objects which were thrown away. Writing from Duleek next day, the Dutch Envoy said in a letter to the States General: "The enemies had retreated in considerable disorder leaving behind guns and baggage, even gold watches and silver dinner services."

William spent the night in his carriage at Duleek. This was a special carriage which he had made and which he brought with him throughout his campaign in Ireland. He summoned his commanders to compliment them for the part they had played in his successful confrontation, and to Count Meinhard Schomberg he had special words of commendation, and commiseration on the death of his father who lost his life fighting so valiantly at Oldbridge.

AFTER THE BATTLE

The next day five battalions of Danes under Brigadier Mellioniere were sent to Drogheda to demand the surrender of the town. The garrison had been under the command of Lord Iveagh, but when he heard of the defeat at Oldbridge he left Drogheda to join the rest of the Jacobites who were fleeing westwards and left the garrison of the town in charge of Brigadier William Tuite. Tuite first of all rejected the call to surrender, but when he saw that Mellioniere had placed his cannon in position to bombard the town he agreed to submit. The garrison marched out without arms, leaving all their baggage behind, however, the officers were allowed to keep their swords. Thus they marched out, leaving Drogheda in Williamite hands, and headed for Athlone to join the final resistance of the Jacobites behind the Shannon.

Also on that day there was an incident which caused some excitement in the vicinity of Duleek. A considerable force of Jacobites appeared nearby - they had come from Munster meaning to join up with James's army, but seeing the great assembly of soldiers in the village they sent two of their number to find out the reason for this. These two unfortunates were seized and hanged, which the rest of the Munstermen seeing, they quickly withdrew and left the place to the Williamites.

On Thursday, July 3 William and his army left for Dublin, and arrived that evening "at a place called Bally Brighan, and there encamped" (Story). On Saturday they marched to Finglas and from their camp there William entered Dublin on Sunday, July 6 where he attended St. Patrick's Cathedral for a "Te Deum" specially celebrated to mark his victory. After this there was great rejoicing among his supporters who ran cheering and shouting through the streets.

THE FLIGHT OF JAMES

As for James we last left him leaving Duleek at about five o'clock on the day of the battle. All during that day Dublin was alive with rumours about the outcome of the event. The French fleet was in Dublin Bay, the Williamites had been defeated, William had been taken prisoner, he had been killed. It was impossible to know what to believe. But about six o'clock in the evening when the first of the Jacobites who had managed to get away from the battle arrived in the city, tired and wounded, there was no longer any doubt about the outcome. James and his bodyguard arrived between nine and ten o'clock that night to put the issue beyond all doubt. There was now a state of panic in the city and many Jacobite families prepared to leave for the west, in order to be out of the way, before the Williamites should arrive.

While James was now determined to leave the country he would not do so without observing the proper protocol. He summoned his advisers, and asked them for their opinions. He was told that he should make haste to leave Ireland to get to France as soon as possible. Having rested himself, he set off next morning at five o'clock accompanied by the Duke of Powis and Henry Fitzjames (his second illegitimate son), and as an escort he retained two troops of his bodyguard. They rode to Bray, where James rested for two hours in the house of a Mr. Hackett, from thence they made their way to Arklow, and after that they rode all night to reach Duncannon in Co. Waterford very early next morning. There they got a boat which brought them to Kinsale, where they got shipping which brought them back to France. Here he hoped that he could still mount a campaign which would restore him to the English throne. It was to be in vain. He died in 1701 without realising his ambition, but the Jacobite cause remained alive as his followers rallied round his son, James Edward, who in an unsuccessful rising in Scotland in 1715 was proclaimed King of England and Scotland. In later years his grandson, Charles (Bonnie Prince Charlie) made a further effort to regain the English throne. The Stuart Cause was finally crushed when Charles and his Scottish followers were defeated at the Battle of Culloden Moor on April 16, 1746.

THE OBELISK

In later years an impressive obelisk was erected at Oldbridge to commemorate the success of the Williamite forces there in 1690. The inscription on it read :

"Sacred to the glorious memory of King William the Third, who on the 1st. of July, 1690, crossed the Boyne near this place to attack James the Second at the head of a Popish army advantageously posted on the south side of it, and did on that day, by a successful battle, secure to us and our posterity our liberty, laws and religion. In consequence of this action James the Second left this kingdom and fled to France. This memorial of our deliverance was erected in the ninth year of the reign of King George the Second, the first stone being laid by Lionel Sackville, Duke of Dorset, Lord Lieutenant of the Kingdom of Ireland, MDCCXXXVI.

"In perpetuam rei tam fortiter quam feliciter gestae memoriam,
Hic publicae gratitudinis Monumenti
Fundamen manibus ipse suis.
Posuit Lionelus Dux Dorsetiae xvii mo. die Aprilis, MDCCXXXVI.
JULY THE FIRST, MDCXC.

This monument was erected by the grateful contributions of several Protestants of Great Britain and Ireland.
Reinard, Duke of Schomberg, in passing this river, died bravely fighting in defence of liberty."
Schomberg was killed during the course of the fighting at a point almost opposite this monument.
The obelisk was blown up on June 2, 1923. Nothing now remains but a few pieces of cut stone on the great rock which bore the monument overlooking the Boyne on the north side of the river.

THE OBELISK

Up to the mid-1970's some stones bearing pieces of the inscription were to be seen in the field around this rock. During land improvements carried out at that time these disappeared - it is presumed that they were buried under the new layer of topsoil that was spread over the area around the rock and towards the river.

Photo taken the day the Obelisk was blown up.

Part of the inscription from the Obelisk plinth.

BIBLIOGRAPHY

THIS ACCOUNT of the Battle of the Boyne has been written using the following sources:

A True and Impartial History, by Rev. George Story. London 1691.

The Beauties of the Boyne and the Blackwater, by Sir W. Wilde, 1849.

The Battle of the Boyne, by D. C. Boulger. Marten Secker, London 1911.

Irish Battles, by G. A. Hayes-McCoy. Longman, London 1969.

The Boyne Water, by P. B. Ellis. Hamish Hamilton, London, 1976.

Eyewitnesses to the Boyne, by J. G. Simms. "The Irish Sword", Vol. 6, No. 22, 1963.

French Eyewitnesses of the Boyne, by Sheila Mulloy. "The Irish Sword", Vol. 15, No. 59, 1982/83.

The Danish Force in Ireland, 1690 - 1691 by Kevin Danaher and J. G. Simms, Dublin, 1962.